HOW TO BE POOR

BY THE SAME AUTHOR

MILO:
HOW
TO BE
POOR

DANGEROUS BOOKS

How to Be Poor

Milo Yiannopoulos

Published by Dangerous Books

This book or parts thereof may not be reproduced in any form, stored in a retrieval system, or transmitted in any form by any means—electronic, mechanical, photocopy, recording, or otherwise—without prior written permission of the publisher.

Copyright © 2019 by Milo Yiannopoulos
All rights reserved

Cover Design: Milo Yiannopoulos
Cover Photo: Mike Allen

CONTENTS

TO JOHN

Thanks to you, no matter what's in my wallet,
I feel like the richest man in the world.

INTRODUCTION

One of the most important things I've ever learned in my life, besides the importance of a good mirror and natural lighting, was taught to me by a drag queen. Long before I developed my own drag character Ivana Wall, a drag queen in London whom I swear to this day was either Justin Trudeau or one of Fidel Castro's other bastard children told me: "Always put your greatest weakness out there yourself, so your enemies can't do it first." Or maybe Eminem taught me that, I don't really remember.

Anyway, Slim and Princess Ketamina, I am going to take your collective advice. I'm going to get the worst thing in my life—the worst thing I can imagine really—out in the open on page one. I, MILO, the mononymous superstar of iconoclast politics, am a very poor person. I don't mean what I would have called poor in 2017, like only reserving rooms for myself and my entourage instead of renting out the entire hotel floor. I don't even mean what *you* may think poor means, like struggling to pay the gas bill each month while the littlest of your ten unfortunate brats can't shake that whooping cough, and Nana's got tuberculosis again.

And I certainly don't mean the special type of poor typical of young liberal voters—the ones who think an occasional shift at the vegan co-op is hard work and who are attempting to run up consumer debt equal to their $200,000 in school loans in pursuit of an advanced degree in menstrual blood painting.

I'm talking about being a destitute, broke-ass son of a bitch. Most Americans will never experience, in fact can hardly dream about, the level of poverty I've fallen into. This is the kind of poor that makes stock-brokers and CEOs take a plunge off a skyscraper. Not because they have actually experienced it, but merely because *they see it possibly coming.* I'm not contemplating such a plunge, in case you are wondering (or secretly hoping for it), but I do try to avoid buildings over three stories tall, so as not to risk the temptation.

My creditors have sent me a series of increasingly hysterical overdue notices. They start with bolding and underlining, then proceed to official-looking stamps on threats of legal action, and have now progressed to dire threats written in blood with entreaties to Satan to strike me down if I don't pay up immediately. You know these types of companies, they always seem to be named after sweet pie-baking old biddies, like the Esther McGillicuddy Corporation of San Antonio, TX—or "Fannie Mae"—and they'll occasionally send along surveillance footage of family members. "Dear Mr. Yiannopoulos, Auntie Suze isn't looking too well. We don't think she'd survive another fall." I'm almost positive these last few letters are written in chicken blood, and not that of innocent children. At least, I hope so. These are after all debt collectors, not Nancy Pelosi sealing a deal to stay alive for just… five… more… years.

My debts are so large they'd make a good number-crunching exercise for an Indian waiting on an H-1B Visa from Donald Trump so he can steal some poor American's job. But it's like I heard someone say on an episode of *Real Housewives of Potomac*, you have to earn a million to owe a million, and although my personal exposure to the disasters of the last few years is minimal, Milo Inc is in the red to the tune of, at last count, over four million dollars. Still, it's not all bad news. Do you know how successful you have to be to end up owing $4 million? You go out and try to get four million in debt. Go on. Tell me how long it takes to get someone to lend you that much money.

Although my first book, *Dangerous*, made me over three million dollars, and although many other ventures over the past few years have been fabulously commercially successful, including multiple sellout tours, there came a time when my earnings began to dry up, while my spending remained the same. And I neither noticed nor cared until it was too late, and not one of the people I hired to manage my affairs had the sense, or courage, to tell me that while Milo was working hard and partying even harder, Milo Inc. was going down the tubes.

I've gone through approximately 265 stages of grief over being poor. Five was not enough. Many of these were variations of shame, which I've always used in the bedroom to get my husband in an appropriately consent-contemptuous frame of mind. But this stuff was very hard to go through. The agony! The humiliation! The certainty of God loving me less as I became one of the impecunious hordes I used to mock.

Many other stages were spent in a haze of substance abuse. I just couldn't comprehend, let alone deal with, the truth, that I was—and am—utterly destitute. Imagine me, with an entire media persona built upon wealth and conspicuous consumption, being *poor*? Even with a long and storied history of men in my rear, I couldn't fathom myself... being in arrears. In other words, I couldn't believe I had been fucked this hard. If I were to take part in a Conservative Model U.N., I'd have to play the part of Liberia. Not because of all the delicious black men there—I'm married now—but because it's the poorest country on Earth. (If you're curious, Ben Shapiro would represent itty bitty little Lichtenstein. Or maybe the Vatican.)

Drag queens are often brutally honest—it's like they put on pounds of make-up but strip away all the niceties we are trained on from birth. So, I will follow their lead with another hard truth: I've been fucked over hard, but, in large part, I was the one doing the fucking. While there is plenty of blame to go around—you have *absolutely no idea* how many snakes there are in the grass until you start making a lot of money, and it is almost impossible to hire a whole company of people who are both competent *and* loyal—I did a lot of the damage myself.

My third big admission—the *coup de grâce*, like the one Hillary's boys delivered to Deputy White House Counsel Vince Foster—is that one of the reasons I am in this predicament is that I am utterly illiterate when it comes to finances. Imagine me, a well-read, intelligent, charming, erudite, down-to-earth intellectual powerhouse being *illiterate* on a topic as simple and as gauche as money? Well, it's true. And don't lecture me about complimenting myself by saying "Pride goeth before a fall," because I've got news for you—pride cometh after a fall too. You'll never take my pride in accomplishing things like leading a campus revolt against ideological brainwashing and helping Donald Trump get elected. Pride is the reason I'm writing this today—because I know I will get back on top, and I want to help you avoid some of my mistakes.

What does financial illiteracy look like? For a decade of my life, the extent of my knowledge about money is that I put my credit card into the machine, and in return I'd be given the most luxurious goods and finest meals. As I'd gain and lose piles of cash, I assumed it was in one of my residences or another of my obscenely expensive wallets. The main interactions with my banks were my frantic calls when I'd wake in the morning to find Lil Hole Punch or Tyrese had pocketed the family silver and I needed a debit card overnighted to me, or the branch manager asking questions about $9,000 spent on strippers and a bouncy castle, only for me to airily inform him that my assistant was enjoying a day off in accordance with standard company policy.

In retrospect, throwing money at fine meals, luxury goods, and the other innumerable categories of stuff and services I wasted my money on were attempts to fill a hole in my heart. No matter how much I bought, I didn't feel that much better. I thought I was rewarding friends as I bought them cars and everything else they wanted, but actually I was temporarily buying surface loyalty and fake praise. Kind of like the rich fat kid in the frat, or Jonah Hill. More on that later. At the height of the madness, Milo Inc. had a Chief Revenue Officer on a vast six-figure salary who brought in zero revenue in six whole months, and a monthly wage bill of over $400,000. I'll never forget being told by my management company and its board of directors to focus on doing good work, and leave the day-to-day numbers to them. And I'll never forget being stupid enough to say: "Sure, okay!"

While I was completely inattentive to my finances, other people were not. All sorts of malcontents, miscreants and rogues found ways into my accounts and the large amounts of cash I would keep on hand. One day these people will get what's coming to them, but again, it was largely my fault for letting them attach to me like leeches. (I know this is captivating reading, but please pause for a moment to leave a comment on my Facebook, if it hasn't been closed down, to guess which blog will be the first to say that line about leeches is anti-Semitic—an allegation that makes no sense, because when Jews steal from you, they know how to cover their tracks. My guess is the *Washington Post*.)

I only began to recover from my spending mania, which shares characteristics with an addiction, thanks to the love and support of my husband John—and by allowing Christianity to become a larger part of my life again. Even then, old habits die hard, and my financial bad habits didn't completely die until my bank account did. Having absolutely no money and massive debts hasn't hurt in prompting me to change my ways—shocker, huh?

This book is intended to give you suggestions, couched with my trademark humor, on how you can live poor, just like me. Done right, being poor is a temporary thing. Don't listen to Bernie, Sandy from the block, and the rest of their privileged fellow pseudo-socialists, who never stop whining about the poor staying poor. It's your decision if you will remain poor, just like it's my decision if I will stay in the gutter. In case you're wondering, there's nothing wrong with slumming to find dates—but as a hobby, not a lifestyle. Either way, I have no intention of staying down. And if you think all this is just a bit sad, and that whole Milo thing is, like, so over, well. Stick around for the last chapter.

I wrote this book for myself. It's the only therapy I can afford, now that I have lost everything. Of course, even when the coffers were overflowing, I'd never have been dumb enough to sign up for actual self-help courses or—shudder—"auditing", because the modern American obsession with finding someone else to blame for your problems has never really appealed to me. Expensive, repetitive, vacuous self-help gurus telling you to take your medication and clean your room are pretty poor substitutes for the confessional booth.

But this book wasn't written only for selfish reasons. Young conservatives need to come to terms with the fact that what has happened to me is happening to others, like my friends Laura Loomer and Alex Jones, and will happen to many others, too, for so long as the Left holds a monopolistic sway on politics and culture. Destroying you is much easier than destroying me, and the Left *will not hesitate* to do so. Eliminating your ability to make an income, blacklisting you and nuking your career prospects are like catnip to progressives, so you must be prepared for a harder life than you deserve, perhaps a harder life than I have had, even if your fall is unlikely to be so precipitous.

This book is also for the lefty bloggers celebrating my downfall. I don't mind them laughing and gloating about either this book or me, because I am completely impervious to their snark and criticism. (You'll find out why later.) In fact, by the time you are reading this, a lot more of them are likely to have been laid off. Lefty blogging, also known as "journalism" just isn't panning out anymore. Their websites are all closing down. Armies of pasty, spindly-armed soy boys are lurching, zombie-like, back to their old Etsy stores. (I first typed that as "Esty," because I'm so constitutionally anti-hipster my fingers refused to even type the name of that website properly.) Even those who aren't laid off will spend the rest of their miserable lives writing smear pieces about high schoolers like the Covington children from a tiny rent-controlled apartment in Brooklyn, hating themselves and everyone they know.

As ever, I welcome any and all feminists reading this book. They'll be dead in their oversize coffins, their surgically-repaired hips and knees finally getting a rest as they are guarded in their eternal slumber by the mummified cats who were their only companions in life, while I'm still in the public eye. I don't begrudge them a bit of *schadenfreude* over my present condition. Enjoy it while you can, bitches. And in a final admission, this book is for anyone that can pay for it. A brother has to eat, even if they are as thin as me. Without further delay, then, it is my great pleasure to reveal to you Milo Yiannopoulos's inimitable guide to being poor.

I

STAYING THIN

There are two types of poor people in America. The short-term poor, like me (and hopefully, you), and the long-term poor. Some people are born poor and remain so their entire lives. It becomes a sort of multi-generational tradition. Yes, there are plenty of true hard-luck cases, but, in general, a lot of poor people in the West need to accept the responsibility for their own circumstances, as I have done. The fact that they will never accept that responsibility is one of the primary characteristics of the long-term poor.

But another primary characteristic of the poor, and the one we must deal with first, is that they are incredibly obese. Some of the most titanic fatties you will ever see are amongst the most impoverished people in this country. I used to be completely mystified by this phenomenon. How do people with less money seem to eat way more food? It's one of capitalism's enduring mysteries. How could they afford to bulk up like the war on poverty had been replaced by the Battle of the Bulge? Staying thin should be easy for poor people but somehow they are still all fat fucking pigs.

Surely poor people were thin in the Victorian era. What happened? I don't remember Oliver Twist being thrown off a jetBlue flight for taking up 32A, 32B and 32C all by himself. Although very few if any Americans are actually suffering from starvation, I expected to see lots of ribs showing among America's poor. I thought I'd shimmy into Target and see bloated bellies like those TV commercials for African charities. But nope. They're just fat. Now that I'm poor, I've come to understand how it happens, and more importantly, how to avoid it. The long-term poor are just as illiterate about nutrition as I used to be about finance. It's a double-whammy, since they don't understand money either.

They guzzle down cheap, processed food, and seemingly make restaurant choices based on how many pounds of food they can buy for under $10, instead of important considerations like ambiance, lighting, and whether the paparazzi will be there. I addressed this in my brilliant *New York Times* bestseller, *Dangerous*, still on sale in all good bookstores, which is as accurate today as it was when it first appeared, just like everything else I have ever written or said.

The Left's embrace of therapy culture has led damaged people to gravitate to the movement. And why wouldn't they? Instead of encouraging people to change themselves, the Left tells vulnerable people that they should instead change the environment around them to protect themselves from having their feelings hurt. 'It's not your fault,' the Left soothingly coos. 'It's society.'

Obesity, a disorder that is as much mental as physical, gets the same treatment. More than a third of adults are obese in the United States, with nearly 70% classified as overweight in some way. Furthermore, health problems caused by obesity are one of the biggest causes of healthcare expenditure, with estimates of the annual cost ranging from $147 billion to $210 billion per year. Obese employees are also estimated to cost employers an extra $506 per obese worker per year. Being fat is damaging to society as well as to the individual.

And what does the Left do in the face of this crisis? Michelle Obama, at least, has campaigned for better diets and active lifestyles for children, even if the meals her campaign produced are disgusting, and systematically thrown away by children. But

> *the radical Left, the intersectional feminist Left, the Left that dreams up new categories of oppression, has responded by declaring that the feelings of fat people are more important than their health."*

The statistics I quoted in *Dangerous* took into account the population overall, including middle-class and wealthy individuals. The long-term poor are much more obese and suffer not only from their own lack of knowledge about nutrition, but also from the Left preaching to them that they have rights as "people of size." For the poor, hearing that they are a special class that deserve special treatment is one of the most seductive forces imaginable. I have come to the conclusion that Big Government—Democrats and cucked Republicans alike—*want* the poor to be obese. There are few other explanations available.

You may protest, pointing out all of the terrible health problems associated with obesity that should be undesirable to any government legitimately representing its citizenry. Things like an inability to work up to their potential or to get around on their own. Placing severe stress on their joints, cardiovascular system, and nearly every other system in their body, leading to lifelong medical care and making themselves so unattractive to potential mates that they are far less likely to copulate and have American babies.

But the evidence is right there in front of us. The Deep State benefits enormously from lethargic, easily controllable citizens who can't turn off CNN unless the remote control is within distance of their reaching aid. We once thought government control was primarily accomplished by dosing people up with ADD, antidepressant and painkilling medication, so they'd be zombies, but it's also done by filling the poor with dollar-menu cheeseburgers.

Feeding vices helps to create an enslaved and compliant population preoccupied with satisfying base urges, which is why governments don't really police pornography. Compare how European police forces treat porn versus how they treat mean words on the internet. They care a lot more about "offensive tweets" than they do about you becoming a dopamine-dependent drone with Pornhub on auto-refresh. One is a sign you might be trouble. The other is a pretty reliable indicator you won't be.

If you are poor and obese, you are at the mercy of Big Government, which keeps the gravy train coming (a literal gravy train, in this case), along with repairing your joints and servicing all your other failing organs. What fatso on government healthcare will vote for a candidate who argues against more spending on health? This may sound like a conspiracy theory, but it's not. It's called "Europe." And it's practically the only explanation that makes any sense for America's nonsensical treatment of the obese poor. We give them credit to buy whatever they want at the grocery store, and, believe me, the other poor people in line ahead of me are buying ice cream and imitation crab meat, not lean mince and lettuce. Why not send them boxed meals, as Donald Trump proposed at one point? We should help the poor to understand that steamed broccoli and grilled chicken will do more for their plight than drowning their sorrows in another milkshake.

You'll notice from the cover of this book and from my videos that despite being poor for over a year, I haven't gained an ounce. That is because, unlike money, I know rather a lot about food, and have spent years being punished over caloric intake by some of the most serious personal trainers around, and also by very mean gay people. I also got fat sucked out of my ass by a plastic surgeon, and it wasn't fun. I'm in no rush to repeat the procedure. If you don't want to fall into the trap of being both broke *and* fat, listen up.

FORGET RESTAURANTS AND BARS EXIST

If you are poor, you should never step inside a restaurant except to put on an apron and wash dishes. Especially if they are serving food of any quality, they are extremely expensive—a massive drain on your tiny monthly budget. Even if the quality is decent, you'll eat far too many calories and carbs, and take in too much saturated fat. By eating at home, you'll spend far less money and eat much better food. This is killing two birds with one stone, as they say in Tehran.

Cutting out restaurants was one of the worst parts of my poverty journey. For people like me, going to a restaurant is less about the food, and more about being seen. Showing off my style and personality over plates of the best food in New York, Los Angeles and Miami was a daily ritual for me, and I have the horrifying receipts to prove it. My tales of restaurant excess are legendary, and widely reported in the media. If a brunch bill came to me for less than $10,000, I thought we must have forgotten to order some dishes. How many people have you met that called a manager over not to complain about being overcharged, but to insist they've been undercharged? I've done it more times than I can count.

More often than not, I'd turn around and post restaurant bills to Instagram to flaunt my wealth. Many of my fans found them obscene, but I didn't understand why. If I'm being completely honest, a part of me still thinks a Sunday afternoon spent in a restaurant is worth a year's rent for a single bedroom apartment in the Midwest, just because it annoys so many people. But most of me has realized the folly of my former ways.

At one of my favorite brunch spots, I bought them special ice cube trays to make capital letter "M" ice cubes out of mineral water from the Welsh hills. They would charge me $400 each Sunday to serve these to my guests. If it was a weekend that I didn't come in, they'd charge me $30 to rent storage space in their freezer, God bless them. Isn't capitalism wonderful?

While the money was there, the wait staff at my favorite haunts lived high on the hog. There's a whole wave of baby Milos born to south Florida waiters grateful to have secured their son's college tuition from my tips. I understand that my money running out is considered such a calamity among the local Cuban population that it almost rivals Fidel Castro giving their parents the boot off their original island home. And the local Trump golf course considered closing down entirely when the headlines hit about my financial cataclysm.

Although I mainly miss the experience of being seen and paying a massive bill for it, I certainly miss the food and drink too. The best champagnes, puddings, and every exotic delicacy you can imagine landed on my plate every day. This is an awful thing to admit, but I still occasionally get the shakes from caviar withdrawal. I wake up in a cold sweat with the taste of the Black Sea in my mouth—a different one than you might expect me to be craving in the middle of the night, but there you are.

The people who believe they are smarter than me will all chime in, "But MILO, what about when you can't get home to cook a meal?" Cool it with the excuses, darlings. All you need to do is some careful planning, something the long-term poor never do. If you know you won't be home, pack a meal. I don't care if it looks silly, you can no longer afford to look cool. There are very few times when you can't pre-pare good quality food at home instead of filling your digestive system with the horrors of corporate food.

Have you ever thought about what is actually in the fast food dollar menu fare you shove down your gullet while smugly thinking about the money you're saving? If they are charging you a buck, it costs them, what 20 cents? It can't be *real* food, can it? Just think about Subway, which everyone thinks is a healthy fast food option. Scientists tested their roasted chicken and found it to be *fifty per cent soy*. Now they want to turn you into a male feminist while they fatten you up! We finally know why Jared Fogle became inter-ested in children. He ate too much Subway chicken.

I have to fight the urge to eat fast food myself. Although I have expensive tastes, I have always loved taking billionaire donors to KFC for fried chicken before asking them for six-figure donations. Alas, I can't even afford a family-sized bucket of KFC today, but I've learned to fry at home, because I am basically black, and that's not because I have no money and a terrible credit score. It's because of osmosis.

SHOP FOR GROCERIES INTELLIGENTLY

If you're eating at home to save money and stay thin, you had better learn to be smart at the grocery store. Somewhere between 50 and 75 per cent of the food in a typical grocery store is just as bad for you as the restaurants you line up for like pigs at the trough. If you don't believe me, look at the front of your local shop. There are almost as many battery-driven hambeast-mobiles as there are shopping carts! America's poor aren't even expected to walk around to pick up their cans of fat. Sad.

The first time I entered a grocery store, I waited for four hours at the front to be greeted and escorted around, only to discover that patrons must go out foraging for goods themselves, as though they are Neanderthal hunter-gatherers. It is a brutal, unforgiving environment, and I'm not just talking about that neon strip lighting. Going to the supermarket for the first time without a supervising adult ranks among the three most stressful experiences of my life, and I lost my virginity in an interracial fivesome with two drag queens.

Much of the modern American grocery store, you will discover, consists of processed fatty foods. These are obviously off the table. MILO critics will say that the poor are forced to eat garbage because it's all they can afford, but that is only true for the terminally lazy. Plenty of raw ingredients like meat and vegetables and pretty much everything else you need are quite reasonably priced. You just have to put a bit more work in. Pork chops are especially affordable and have the added advantage of warding off the Religion of Peace if you cook them often enough.

Pig is powerful. Those Jews need never have stayed home on 9/11—they should have just asked the goyim in the next cubicle to fry up some gammon. No self-respecting al-Qaeda terrorist would have risked flying into the towers only to be denied his virgins because he took his last breath in a pungent soup of unignited jet fuel and hickory-scented bacon grease. I'm just saying!

Illegal aliens are able to afford a metric fuckton of groceries to feed their massive families working for less than minimum wage. That means you can feed yourself nourishing meals too—by avoiding the junk food.

Here's another fact to face. Our culture wastes a

ton of food, and you need to seize the financial advantage in that waste. I'm not suggesting you should dumpster dive for meals. Even I'm not poor enough to go into rubbish bins looking for lunch. But grocery stores regularly mark down expiring food to clear it out. Old meat is your friend—and the steaks are much more tender that way. I can hear you protesting from here. Honey, get over yourself. If you don't want to stay poor, you stretch every dollar as far as you can when it comes to food. I've learned the bitter lesson that whether the steak costs $600 at Michael Mina or $2.50 on mark-down, it still ends up a giant stinking turd.

DON'T STOP WORKING OUT

I've focused this chapter on food and drink, because fast food is like burning money for the poor. But as you tighten the belt on food expenses, it is critical to remember the other side of the equation: exercise. Regular exercise will not only improve your physical health, it will also help you momentarily forget the crushing burden of being poor in America, and make you sleep better without other things you can't afford, like booze and drugs. The key is to exercise cheaply, just like everything else in your new life as a poor person.

You can certainly find ways to exercise for free, like jogging in a park or engaging in some physical labor. If you really need some motivation, I suggest putting on your running shoes, finding your local Black Lives Matter rally, slapping on your MAGA hat and shouting into the crowd about black-on-black crime rates. Give yourself a ten-second head start as the mob assembles to chase you through the streets. There's that ideal we are always aiming for again— two women with one stone.

A modest gym membership is well worth the cost, and you should be able to cover it based on drastically cutting back on food expenses. Cheap gyms operate on the business model of people signing up and then hardly using the facilities, so if you hit the gym every day, you'll enjoy the added bonus of sticking it to the man. But here's an important side note: no degree of penury or excessive weight can ever justify being spotted at CrossFit. It's just too gay.

If you like to keep your exercise regimen purely recreational, consider that the average male burns 4.2 calories, and the average woman 3.1 calories, per minute of sex. Ladies! If you want to shed those last few vanity pounds, you know what to do. Ride 'em, cowgirl!

The food you take in, and the exercise you do to burn it off, are key contributors to your health and your financial future. Whenever you're tempted by a restaurant commercial or a pleasant aroma wafting out of a sidewalk cafe, just imagine me telling you, "Put down the fork, fatty," in a cross tone of voice— it's completely free. See? I'm saving you money already.

II
GETTING AROUND

Now that we've addressed how proper food management can both save you a ton of cash and keep you from turning into a hamplanet, we can move on to a second major area of spending to cut back on: transportation. America, I love you dearly, but your transportation system is a fucking mess. It may be the only mess in this country outside of AOC's perpetually refilled diaper that is as bad as my current balance sheet.

Plenty of Americans live in places with almost no public transportation to speak of. Where there is public transportation, it is often a crappy way to get around—always running late, frequently breaking down, and the people on the bus are as poor as you, but way crazier and considerably more fragrant. This is due in part to America's obsession with the automobile. I'm not really criticizing this obsession, by the way. It has seized my soul just like most Americans.

But for us poor folk, a shiny new car in the driveway isn't only impractical, it's often impossible. I used to have no idea what a credit score was—I thought your FICO score went up the more pieces of Louis Vuitton luggage you owned. Now I know all about it, and I can authoritatively say I'd only get approved for a car loan if the finance manager had Down syndrome, like poor Dave Rubin.

I've primarily lived in big cities in America. I couldn't dream of utilizing public transportation in Los Angeles or Miami, imagine the riff-raff! So, my life revolved around a series of cars. Except I never drove—I didn't know how—it's just not the done thing for a well-heeled young Englishman to drive himself around. I should point out before we continue that even though I am now poorer than a Sarah Lawrence graduate, I still would never take the bus in New York City, because if you're white and can operate a pen and paper, you're not allowed. As a firm believer in equality I know that segregation is wrong, which is why we need a Rosa Parks for middle-class white people in New York. Except her name will be Becky or Debbie.

I used to rent cars like a mad bastard. My entourage couldn't fit in a single Escalade, so we'd keep multiple vehicles on hand, often for weeks at a time. I couldn't tell you how much it cost. It just went onto my American Express Platinum like everything else. And rental cars were just the start. I used to compete with myself to break my personal record for the number of Uber Lux trips taken in one day. I never got higher than 15 trips in a single 24-hour period, but I often came close. I was such an early and enthusiastic adopter of Uber that I've heard they once considered me their top customer. Lyft tried to woo me away, but I wanted nothing to do with them. Uber drivers might turn out to be rapists alarmingly often, but I'm convinced Lyft is for hippies and pedophiles.

I didn't use Uber only to transport myself around whatever town I was in, I also used it as a convenient way to dispose of those I was done with, back when I was single. Almost like concierge human refuse removal. As I explained in my smash hit book *Dangerous*: "I've lost count of the number of black guys I've personally lifted out of poverty. (Admittedly, I send them back the next day in an Uber.)" I also wouldn't settle for just any Uber. Whenever possible, I'd pay through the nose for Uber Black service. I was always out to impress my companions with luxury, even if it was for a 20-minute ride in a car that didn't belong to me. In Los Angeles, every Uber Black driver knew me on sight, and would fight over the chance to shuttle me around. This felt familiar, because I'm used to being fought over by black men. But even the straight ones wanted me in their cars!

Another of my well-known Uber hang-ups is that I refused to be a passenger in a car driven by a woman. Some risks are just not worth taking, you see, and I'm saying that as a friend of Chadwick Moore, the gay journalist notorious for regularly engaging in unprotected sex with strangers in airport bathrooms while intoxicated.

No matter how complex Uber's algorithms got, they never seemed to get the message that I only wanted male drivers. Uber is infamous for creating software to cheat world governments or crush competition by starving them of drivers. I have it on good authority that they developed a program to track what city I was in and make sure multiple female drivers were close to me at all times knowing that I'd piss away money on the cancellations ($10 a time).

I've paid so many cleaning fees to Uber, I've probably cleaned the car of every driver they've ever had. My dog handler would catch an Uber to take the dog to the park less than a mile away and it would shit on the back seat, or the boys drunk on my tab would throw up, or piss all over some poor sap's car. I was almost suspended from Uber over all the messes we made, which is the only reason I finally put my foot down... by hiring a fleet of Escalades.

But my love affair with Uber never wavered until my credit cards stopped working. After that, all of these drivers who would warmly greet me every day stopped showing up. It turns out Uber drivers are only in it for the money—most of my former friends were, too, but at least Uber is honest about it.

Although I always rode in Ubers or was chauffeured by my crew in hired Escalades, in 2017 I dabbled in purchasing cars. The first few cars I bought were for members of my squad. I've always been a soft touch. One got a truck, another got a sports car. I thought these young fellows were good guys and loyal to me, so if I just got them the car of their dreams then perhaps they would become *useful* in some way, returning value for value. Of course—as you can predict—that didn't happen. They continued to leave the doors of my home wide open, trash a beachfront mansion I rented for them at the cost of $10,000 a month, and leave loaded firearms lying around with the windows open. Why would they care about any of that? It was me who'd get in trouble.

The first car I bought for my own family was the most ostentatious thing I could find—a gold Tesla Model X P100D—which was, to my knowledge, the only one in the world. It cost over $200,000. It was my gift to my soon-to-be husband John. He'd never had anyone buy him a car, and I was determined to do it the right way. I don't regret the purchase at all, because it was for him. As crazy as it sounds, it was the most sensible $200,000 I spent in the last decade. But I sometimes wonder if that car was the beginning of my misfortune, in some way. Maybe God looked down and saw me with a bull in a golden car and put it in the same category as worshipping a golden calf. Even if that is the case, I don't begrudge God his judgment, or my misfortune.

Although that car was paid for in cash, saving me from the ignominy of having it repossessed by creditors—or having Elon Musk tweet about my outstanding balance—it joined the fire sale of my assets as I tried to keep my head above water. One day, I will have another gold Tesla, or save money by buying the first one back. See how I'm changing? I actually said "save money" out loud!

Having documented some of my travel foibles, I'll now recover a bit of dignity by giving you some travel tips:

#NEVERUBER

Pretend taxi apps don't exist. And don't cheat by going back to regular taxis either! Uber, Lyft, and anyone else that gets into the rideshare game will suck every penny out of your wallet that restaurant and bars don't. You can't afford them. Leave them all behind. If it makes you feel any better, these companies are run by Leftist Silicon Valley pricks of the highest order. Starve them back! Find alternatives to these services. For one thing, stop being poor and lazy and just walk. There's no law that says you have to be in the back of a comfortable Uber to get anywhere. Humans have walked around for thousands of years. I think you can deal with a few miles a day.

You can also buy a bike second hand for the price of an Uber fare or two and pedal your way to fitness at the same time. You might feel like a Chinese peasant riding around roads filled with cars, but the peasant probably has a higher net worth than you. Look—you have several different options, but the main idea is that you can no longer afford to pay men (or women, if you're suicidal, or immigrants, if you want to get raped) to drive you from point A to point B every day.

SWALLOW YOUR PRIDE

If you live in a city with a remotely functional form of public transportation, bite the bullet and get on the train or bus. Yes, yes, I just talked about how horrid public transportation is, but you have to come to the realization—quickly—that your life will oftentimes have to be temporarily horrid if you don't want to stay in the hole forever.

Bring a book to keep yourself occupied and to accomplish something during the ride. Never make eye contact. Let me repeat, never make eye contact! I'm sure some readers in Iowa are smirking at this as one of my exaggerations, but they are welcome to visit New York City's subway system anytime they please. Bring mace and disinfectant.

People to whom I've given advice about public transportation have complained that it isn't convenient to their home or work. Just be creative for once! You are all good at puzzles and video games. Apply that part of your brain to real-life conundra. If the issue is getting to the train or bus and then from there to work, find options. Beg a ride if necessary, or join a carpool to the station that lets you chip in a little for gas and parking.

SOMETIMES, CARS ARE NEEDED

As I mentioned at the beginning of this chapter, America is a country in love with the automobile. Much of the population lives in places where the only practical method of transit is a car, instead of public transportation, or even walking and biking. If you live in one of those places, you need one.

So, the question becomes how to own and operate a car when you're poor. Like many things in life, there is an easy way and a hard way. The easy way keeps you poor. The mistake the vast majority of poor people make is to purchase a car far beyond their financial means that they will owe money on *forever.* Car dealerships, like most lenders, are perfectly happy to lend you more money than you can afford to pay. They just jack up your interest rate and watch you squirm. Eventually you have a $20,000 loan at a usurious interest rate on a car worth $4,500.

Instead, you need to buy a hooptie. A hooptie is the shittiest car you can find that still has four wheels, an engine, and brakes. Everything else is superfluous, although I am open to a debate on seatbelts. This car will not be pretty, and it probably won't last very long. Your goal is to milk it for every ounce of utility, just as those surrounding me milked me for every penny. You also can't treat this car as the typical woman does, nor as you treat the typical woman, ignoring all maintenance and TLC. In fact, you had better find a handy neighbor, parent, or friend that can take care of little problems for you. Or watch a lot of YouTube videos on repairs.

You'll be best off getting a high mileage Japanese car like a Honda or Toyota. American cars at high mileage are piles of junk. Maybe it's the union labor. Who knows. With some gentle driving, your beater doesn't have to be a deathtrap or leave you stranded on the side of the road. (Note: American cars are much cheaper to repair, parts cost less, and most basic repairs can be done with hand tools by even a modestly skilled amateur YouTube instructed "mechanic." Japanese cars typically require specially trained technicians, computer diagnosis of mechanical issues, and the parts are much more expensive.)

Whatever else you do, don't make the mistake of most people who dig their way out of the poorhouse and promptly pick up a fancy new car with a big loan. You can certainly upgrade, but no gold Teslas.

III

YOUR HAIR

Earlier in this book I said that my wealth has been a core component of my persona. It isn't the only component—there's being British, hilarious, and of course my debate skills and sense of style. But, above all else, there is The Hair.

I believe this is an appropriate moment to announce that I no longer identify as a gay man. Gay is boring—the most ideologically cucked group of fags that ever existed. Instead, I am now identifying as two-spirit, in the American Indian tradition. Most two-spirits are little more than trannies with some spiritual mumbo-jumbo thrown in. I prefer a literal definition—there are two spirits inhabiting me. MILO, and MILO's hair. Or maybe it's MILO, and BELOW MILO'S ROOTS. I'm still working this all out. But feel free to use my "scalpself" pronoun. And please, spare me any grief for appropriating American Indian culture. I'm at least as injun as Liz Warren.

There is plenty of precedent for the hair being as important as the man. It's in the Bible after all. I'm just a modern-day Samson. He got strength from his hair; I get cunning, charisma, and the ability to charm the socks off even the most diehard Leftist. I've given you this long-winded setup, so you understand nothing in my life is as important as my hair. It's taken me everywhere I've ever gone, from Father Michael's lap to the pinnacle of worldly fame. Considering how much money I've thrown at things I don't care about, can you even imagine how much money I've spent on what I hold most dear?

This is yet another thing, by the way, that I have in common with the African-American community, besides an inexplicable fondness for Wendy Williams and the fact that I was raised by my grandmother. You see, generationally-poor urban blacks understand the importance of hair care. Not so much rural whites, though I love you guys too, and I especially love that you TRY.

Poor urban blacks take great pride in their hair and nails, and this is why they are better than you. You can't swing a dead tranny in the hood without hitting Yolanda's African Queen Beauty Emporium, or a barbershop filled with hulking studs getting a fade every

Friday night. There are probably more beauty salons in the hood than any other business—including ice cream trucks selling crack cocaine to toddlers.

Not everyone does such a bang-up job. Illegals are at the bottom of the hair tree. Judging by the news footage they slap on a shit-stained baseball cap they found in the sewer with a logo printed on the front that they can't even read. We don't need to cover what poor Jews do with their hair, because there aren't any poor Jews.

I talked about part of my haircare routine in *Dangerous*, but it was cut out of the final manuscript, one of my greatest professional mistakes, besides going broke of course. My editor said the book was running long and had far too many masturbatory asides about how great my life was, which I had presumed when I signed the deal was the whole point of the book. He also said it read like a character in a Bret Easton Ellis novel, the highest compliment I've ever been paid, since Bret, who is now a friend of mine, basically invented Milo 1.0 in *American Psycho*. I can finally rectify that mistake by revisiting a portion of my morning routine here. I've narrowed it down solely to the passage about my hair.

After washing and conditioning with something called Russian Amber, I blow dry my hair enough to apply a moisturizing base texturizer followed by a harder wax, usually one from Aveda. I use a softer finishing cream from the same brand to add shine and glossiness, and a new hairspray I found in a boutique salon in East London. It has a French name that no one reading this book can pronounce properly, so I won't bother to tell you it, but it holds the hair in place without residue. Plus, it's placenta-free, which is why you don't find it on sale in Beverly Hills.

I used to repeat this routine every time I took a shower. With my sex life, that added up to a lot of showers. I really have no way to tell you how much I was spending on my haircare products at that time, because I'd just wave one of my cards and the shops would load me down with packages. All I know is that my hair looked like a million bucks—perhaps one of the few times that perception matched cost.

My personal hair care regimen was really just the start of expenses related to my hair. The types of salons I frequented charged an unholy sum for even the most basic services. A blow-dry and style might cost forty or fifty times what a normal American man spends on a proper haircut. I've spent the type of money in salons that would make Bruce Jenner fall into an envious and manly rage. The only way I knew I was in an appropriate salon was if there were no prices posted. If you have to ask, you belong in a barbershop.

On the Dangerous Faggot college tour, the budget had a line item for my salon visits. I believe it was the third largest individual line item, after the bus and hotel rooms in each city. In fact, my salon expenses during the tour were so high, my superiors suspected they were being used to hide all manner of illicit purchases. They had an accountant track through every receipt only to discover that every dime had in fact been spent on my hair. I believe my single most expensive salon visit cost $2,000, although that included make-up and a massage, so that might be considered cheating. The chief stylist at that salon, Paolo, is a genius. He's the gay Leonardo da Vinci of Rodeo Drive.

As an aside, hair stylists are one of the few classes of people who seem to easily cross the political divide. Of course they are all Leftists—it's gay men and clueless women, what do you expect? But even the most ardent Leftist stylist cannot help but love a good head of hair and mine, as I can confidently say because all of America knows it to be true, is magnificent. Despite my politics, and even me pointing out Leftist lunacy while in the chair, most stylists can't help but fall in love with me. I actually wonder how many I've turned away from the Left just by letting them get their grateful and reverential hands on my head, and of course leaving a healthy tip.

By now, you can understand that hair care became one of the primary drains on my finances, just like food and getting around. Of all the expenses in my life that I had to drastically cut back, haircare was by far the toughest. It was profoundly damaging to my psyche to know that I could no longer purchase the very best products and care for my hair, my second spirit.

Many of you would not feel this way about your hair. But imagine something you hold as close to your heart. Perhaps your car, or a gun collection, or even a gaming computer. The sinking feeling that you can no longer maintain something you love at the extravagant level to which you've become accustomed is devastating. But all is not lost. You can manage to be presentable without spending much. If you are a man, you're already accustomed to spending far less than me. Female readers, of which there are plenty, are much more likely to understand my pain and the difficulty of cutting back. Here is the MILO guide to maintaining good hair even when you're poor.

BUZZ IT ALL OFF

One thing to consider is going for a buzz cut. This is cheap to maintain and you can do it yourself. Plenty of guys look really cute with buzzed hair too—it's so butch! I always prefer stubble to a clean-shaven head, but that sort of detail I'll leave up to you.

On my darkest days, I've considered buzzing my hair off, if only to troll the fans who care more about my hair than me. Young people would make memes of me with an eye patch and scars labeled "Punished MILO" after one video game or another. Gays would make references to Britney Spears' darkest days. But then I come to my senses and remember I wouldn't buzz my hair off for a million dollars. After all, a million dollars would hardly put a proper dent in my debts. Maybe for $20 million.

PHONE A FRIEND

Take a clue from black culture and get a friend in your circle that can cut hair. Every group of black men has a barber in their midst. Sure, you may not get the very best cut in the world, but it's better than nothing, and you don't want to end up with a man bun, do you?

One of the best ways to do this is to just be friends with a professional stylist. An upcoming chapter will focus on the utility aspect of friendship, but this is a good place to point out that if your friend cuts hair for a living, they can give you a decent cut at a low price or perhaps for free. Even if you have no hope of being friends with a stylist, most likely one of your friends can do a decent job with a pair of scissors. At least enough to keep you from getting dirty looks during a job interview.

RISK A TRAINEE

Odds are you live close to a beautician school, trainee barbershop, or other business that teaches people to cut hair. You can get really cheap haircuts here, at the grave risk of a complete disaster when a nervous first-timer makes you look like the twat from Prodigy who just croaked. A lot of people say it's worth the risk. You can get a real haircut for a laughably low price, and if you care about helping others, you can tell yourself you assisted the trainee in improving their skills. I imagine if the cut is really going South, the instructors will step in and fix things. But don't quote me.

SPLURGE ONCE IN A WHILE

I have to admit I wouldn't touch any of these options, even with my husband's ten-foot pole. It took me a long time to develop the trust to let anyone besides a highly paid professional even come close to me with a hair dryer. My hair is *me*. So, I occasionally still splurge by spending on a decent salon. I don't go to the top-end places I'm used to, but rather a sensible salon that sets me back about $75. I find the stylists are so thrilled to work on my immaculate hair that they pull out all the stops, nearly matching the more exclusive places.

It also helps that I am not visiting the salon four times a week now. Only once, unless I turn up some extra cash and double up. I never claimed to be perfect at saving money, just much better than I used to be. Besides, I could get my hair taken care of *eighty times* for the price of one MILO brunch back in the day. Baby steps!

IV
PICKING NEW FRIENDS

In this book I've talked about some of the terrible drains on personal finance that I—and every person who doesn't want to be in the poorhouse for the rest of their lives—have to fix, pronto. Yes, we all have to eat and have adequate transportation to survive. Some of us also have to have stunning hair to make it through our day.

These are all necessities of varying degrees of importance, but it's time I address another aspect of life that is considered a necessity by most humans— friendships. Friends help us get through the day, pick us up when we are down, and provide motivation to look better, dress better, and be smarter and funnier than they are around potential sex partners.

Friends are also an absolutely terrifying drain on personal finances. As you reconfigure your daily life to work yourself out of the *broke motherfucker* category, to use the technical lingo of the finance industry, you will have to develop an entirely new group of friends. The sad fact is your friends helped you end up where you are today, just like they did for me.

Even before my rise to intergalactic fame, my life was overflowing with friends and prospective friends desperate to break into my social circle. This exploded as I entered the American stage in full force starting in 2014. My ego, which is larger than several of Jupiter's moons, convinced me that these people wanted to be my friend because of my stunning looks, dazzling charm, and devotion to defending those without a voice in the mainstream media.

I learned the hard way that I was blinded by vanity. As my stock shot up, the friends I attracted came to me with largely selfish intentions. They wanted to attach themselves to my fame. They wanted to live off my credit cards. Many of them, above all else, simply wanted access and social cachet. They wanted my stamp of approval on their products and services and they wanted their websites shared with my audience. By 2017, as an established superstar in the political world, I attracted more old-fashioned grifters eager to suck money out however they could. Some of the friends I'd gained in recent years converted into this type of monster as well—even some long-term friends from Europe ended up this way. They were all vampires draining my blood bank.

If my life were a horror movie—which it feels like much of the time—the plot would center around me being a carrier of the vampire virus, yet immune to it. Anyone who touched my finances would turn into a heartless monster whose thirst could only be slaked by MILO's money, and I wouldn't figure out how to detect these vampires until it was too late. You must admit, me being a disease carrier really lends some credibility to the scenario—whether my haters are on the control-left or the alt-right, they are all convinced by my gravity-defying cheekbones that I am pozzed, which is gay slang for "too poor to buy rubbers and too lazy to go to the clinic."

In *Dangerous*, I reflected on the support I received from friends during one of the many times my enemies thought they had killed me. What feels like a million years ago, I wrote: "These have been trying times and I have been tested. There were a few days when I almost gave up on my mission. But thousands of fans reached out, my friends and family had my back, and the people of this world I respect the most kept taking my calls. I couldn't let you all down. My enemies thought I had been vanquished, that I would go into hiding in the hills of Dartmoor with my dick between my legs like some weak ass pussy faggot. They couldn't be more wrong. All they've done is piss me off."

That passage has remained true for some of my more recent problems, including my financial fall from grace. For my sincere fans and friends, I thank you for sticking with me, and for purchasing this book. One thing is for sure, going broke absolutely separates those out for a quick buck from one's actual mates. To understand my relationship with friends, and how it got me into trouble, you have to grasp my system. The old saying goes, "Make new friends, but keep the old, one is silver and the other gold," which I adapted slightly into my own credo: "Make new friends, then rank them according to their personal qualities and let them fight to earn your favor."

MY SPREADSHEET

To pick up a thread I mentioned at the beginning of this chapter, even before making it big in America, there was a massive demand to make my friends' list in Europe. This isn't some vague metaphorical concept, where the young and upwardly mobile hoped to be my friend. They actively worked to become an entry on my friends spreadsheet, where I tracked friends across many variables, such as their dress sense and likelihood of getting into trouble with the law.

I became notorious for these annual ratings, which were covered by an astonished and slightly scared media. Those rated highly lorded it over those who had slipped in the rankings, and hipsters who couldn't make the list typed scathing blogs about me while blinking back salty, skinny-fat tears. I wielded my spreadsheet like a weapon. My ratings were (and are) technically secret, but every now and then I would strategically mention to someone they were climbing the ranks—or falling. I clearly remember how devastated certain people were to learn they didn't even warrant an entry, despite thinking we were close.

I explained the MILO power rankings in a column for the *Kernel,* a website I founded and later sold: "I rank pretty much everyone I meet that I might want to see again in a number of different ways: subjective cultural assessments, estimates of income and intelligence, how much they like to party, how much trouble they like to get into, and obviously, how physically attractive they are.

"The scores are normalized across the whole group. This enables me quickly and easily to drill down and generate lists from which I can craft the perfect party.

I can even engineer how the photos will look, since I have a column that covers personal style. Politics is covered by a simple 'Pass' or 'Fail.' "

Typically, when my enemies comment on my notorious spreadsheet, they treat it as sociopathic. How on Earth could someone keep rankings of their friends? But it isn't sociopathic at all, it's just good sense. Okay, there is one *slightly* sociopathic aspect of my spreadsheet—I treated my friends like stocks that I would go long on, meaning invest my time into deepening the friendship, or sell short, meaning avoid or sabotage. As I wrote back in the day: "I won't pretend I don't get a frisson of childish amusement from 'shorting' the 'stock' of people who show up late for an appointment (I'm hoping to commission a mobile app so I can do that on the fly) or even demoting those who have annoyed me in some way."

You see, successful people operate based on facts and data, also known as "facts before feelings." Unsuccessful people operate almost completely on emotion. And this is true for the long-term poor as well. Their emotional decision making reinforces every negative aspect of their lives. I was just trying to think for the long term.

There was just one problem with my spreadsheet as it existed from 2010 until its radical reinvention in 2019. The qualities that I cared about, and how I quantified those qualities for analysis purposes, were deeply flawed. One inexorable fact of data analysis is this: if you put garbage in, you'll get garbage out. And what I put in was a very particular kind of garbage. The self-serving kind. For example, what I measured when I estimated my friends' intelligence was actually *how smart they made me feel.*

After all, high IQ people can kill a party. If they aren't autistic, they are still often odd. They can kill a conversation by being too smart, and scare away the girls so vital for getting hunky straight guys to show up. Likewise, I was estimating the wealth of my friends despite being financially illiterate myself. Doubtless on many occasions I rated friends as wealthy when they were practically as broke as I am now, and vice versa.

I put far too much credence on my special rating for how much trouble a friend was likely to get in (or cause) because I valued mischief highly. Inevitably, that mischief most often came at my own expense. It's amazing what some people are willing to destroy when they don't have to pay the repair bill, isn't it? As my fame increased, multiple new variables entered the spreadsheet, muddying the water. Would this friend make me look better to Americans? Is this friend so handsome they may draw the spotlight away from me in some social circumstances? That last one was a wonderful way to plunge to the bottom of the spreadsheet, by the way.

The end result of following my spreadsheet was a devotion to the worst people in my life. The best-dressed people led me into an arms race of $20,000 handmade jackets and accessories. The troublemakers blew through my money in repair bills. The hard luck cases got cars and rent payments and everything under the sun. The gourmands joined my fabulous (and fabulously expensive) chef's tables in the finest restaurants. The best looking got all this and more. And I got a top rank of friends, my elite praetorian guard, who disappeared when the money ran out. If only I had tracked "likelihood to turn against MILO at the drop of a hat."

BITCH, I'M BRAND NEW

In a fake celebrity book, this is the part where the Hollywood star would explain that they've changed their ways, they've seen the light and they no longer track friends on a spreadsheet. That's all bullshit—when a celeb says that, they mean they fired their personal assistant and got a better one to track their friends for them. I still have my spreadsheet, but I've learned from my mistakes. I don't track my friends based on how cool or wealthy they are, because all that does is make me spend money trying to keep up appearances of superiority. Instead, I track what my friend's actual interest in me is, and more importantly, what they can do for me. I also keep tabs on what I can do for them.

As I look back on my pre-2019 rankings, a profile for a group of friends well down the list—almost to the point of obscurity—emerged. These people had good politics, little to no fashion sense, were not in the top 50 per cent of my friends based on looks, were very smart, and were willing to help me out on projects large and small. They also typically had good networks of trustworthy individuals to help out on problems. These people didn't betray me and didn't disappear on me through any of my various and sundry scandals.

This core has evolved into a new ranking of MILO's friends, which values fidelity and usefulness over coolness and troublemaking. This may sound drearily middle-aged to some of you, but when you're broke you have to come to terms with maturity and responsibility, or you're going to stay broke forever. You will have your own way of doing this, but the bottom line is: Get better friends.

START YOUR OWN SPREADSHEET

My advice to you is to start your own spreadsheet.
You don't even need to pay. You can run the whole
thing in a Google spreadsheet like I do. I wouldn't
worry about Mountain View knowing who your
friends are, they already know what you jerk off to.
And your friends list isn't valuable to them until you
are no longer poor.

Rate your friends on things that matter: honesty,
fidelity, will they screw you over, will they rat you
out to the police. You know, the actually important
things in life. Don't rank them on looks, coolness at
a party, and how they act over dinner or drinks, or
you'll end up just like I did—flat broke and with a
bad list. Since you're currently poor, you should add
some columns that seem awfully mercenary, but are
really about survival. Can this person drive you places
for free? Do they have a special skill you can utilize,
like cutting your hair? Do they have a place for you to
crash when you're dodging creditors? Will they pick
up the check for a splurge meal?

In my case, friends were one of the worst things
that ever happened to my pocketbook, because I
chose friends for the wrong reasons and my data-
driven approach to friendship had fatal flaws in its
logic. In your case, this same approach with construc-

tive criteria can help you save tons of money while also building meaningful attachments that can last a lifetime.

V
PUTTING OUT

Once you're poor, you feel like you've lost everything. Congratulations, for once your feelings are correct. Well, *almost* correct. You still have your body, and that in itself is a form of currency as old as humanity. In this chapter, I'd like to give you some tips about using your sexuality to get yourself out of the hole. Perhaps a poor choice of words—but desperate times call for desperate measures. Some of you are already gritting your teeth and getting ready to kick the shit out of me for suggesting you become a rent boy—but it's not quite as bad as that. I'm not suggesting anyone turn queer just because they are broke.

But straights can apply some of the same techniques as gays (and women) and even if you don't go the sexual route, you can still sell your body in today's economy. And it turns out that if you want to *really* take advantage of your sexuality, you don't need to charge a thing. Read on.

SEX: NATURE'S CRYPTOCURRENCY

Long before Bitcoin—or *any* coins for that matter—sex was a currency for humankind. It's the original form of barter. I'm sure there are cave paintings of young men trading their ass for a hunk of roasted woolly mammoth. In the western world, we don't think of sex the same way any longer. Streetwalkers have been normalized as "sex workers," as if they punch a time card at some penile conveyor belt and hobble off bow-legged with a metal lunch box halfway through their shift.

But the role of sex as currency is fundamentally unchanged throughout history. This is clearest when we study the most disadvantaged people in the western hemisphere, illegal immigrants from Central America. Women and even young girls pay with their bodies to illegally come to America. They might not know it, but their families certainly do, which is why we see widespread reports of women and girls armed with contraceptives to avoid pregnancy during their journey through Mexico.

According to one report by Splinter, something like 80 per cent of women and girls attempting to enter America illegally from Central America will be raped or sexually assaulted. Splinter is owned by Univision, so it's not like a pro-Trump, pro-wall organization is putting out this information. One woman quoted in the *New York Times* talked about being raped in Mexican brothels on her way to America: "They just told us, 'You guys don't have money, so you have to pay with your body.'"

Splinter explained that this is not the exception, it is the rule. "The arrangement is so common there's a slang term for it—'cuerpomátic,' or 'cuerpomático' (an apparent wordplay on Credomatic, a Central American credit-card processing firm), which means to use one's body, or cuerpo, as a source of currency." The American government knows exactly what is going on. DHS Secretary Kirstjen Nielsen testified to Congress that every Central American woman gets a pregnancy test at the border because sexual assault is so common. As if that wasn't bad enough, the same rule applies to any girl over the age of ten.

For any leftist bloggers reading this book, this is your signal to stop reading and quote the above for your outrage piece on me. I imagine you will say I'm in favor of these poor women and girls being raped by Mexicans and their globalist friends in this country. Go ahead and type up your post, I'll still be here when you get back. For the rest of you:

of course I am against the rape, sexual assault, and sexual exploitation of *anyone*. Well. Anyone except cyclists, vegans and atheists. The treatment of women and girls illegally entering America is one of the best arguments to build a massive wall to stop the flow. I honestly can't decide if the leftists that oppose the wall simply don't know or block out information on sexual assault, or if they are the customers of sex trafficked women and children. Sorry, I think I got lost on a tangent, but that's how much I want Daddy to build his big, beautiful wall.

MAKING YOUR SEXUALITY WORK FOR YOU

I'm not suggesting you sell yourself in a Mexican brothel. I'm also not suggesting you become a "sex worker" on the street or with an outcall service. This type of sexual behavior opens you up to disease, exploitation, and above all else, violence. I have traded sex in the distant past for large sums of money, and I have been in the room when it all goes wrong. I have also seen young men nearly beaten to a pulp by johns who didn't enjoy "feeling like a faggot" utilizing the services of a 19-year-old male escort. Gay prostitutes have it worse than the women, despite what any feminists tell you. It's called rough trade for a reason.

Even without full-blown sex work, straight men can leverage their sexuality into badly-needed currency. Women and gay men have always understood this, while most straight guys are blissfully unaware. Well, if you're poor, you can't afford to be unaware any more. There is an emerging class of women with some money but without male company. Call them cougars, call them "wine aunts," but feminism's negative influence on our culture has left a lot of women working a job with nothing to spend all that dosh on, besides of course wine and Ben & Jerry's. Sometimes they want company.

There is no reason young, handsome straight men reading this cannot become a sugar mommy's boy-toy for however long it takes to get back on their feet. MILF porn is absurdly popular in America, so don't try to tell me you couldn't get it up for a woman with a few wrinkles. Girls and gays have done this forever. Feminism has shifted the balance of sex to the point that there are more lonely women than there were in the past, which poor straight men should capitalize on. Of course, it is still infinitely easier for gays and girls to exploit the lonely moneyed men that favor them, but this option is more open than ever before.

You might also consider entering the edges of the smut world without diving in too deep. Every stripper claims to be doing it just to pay for college, but very few of them leave the club. Every other area of selling sex is the same way, so you must be very careful, but you can monetize sex without sucking a stranger's dick in a random car. In fact, the best ways involve no contact with strangers at all.

For example, why should streaming video be the exclusive fiefdom of thots and titty streamers? These girls make thousands of dollars playing dance games on Twitch or painting their bare breasts. Why not crash their action with your own shirtless videos? If you stream your daily exercise routine, you can improve your physique while making tips. Of course, you will do so with the knowledge that your audience is mostly closet cases jerking off to your sweaty shoulders, but whatever.

If you're presentable and have a willing sexual partner, you might even dabble in cam porn. This is the only form of porn that is still relatively safe, although it can have negative repercussions on your future career when your coworkers find out what you did. And they will find out. Every sex video ever posted to the Internet has been found, with the exception of my video from a weekend on the French Riviera with an imam, four Norwegian flight attendants, and a mechanical bull with its warranty well and truly voided.

Finding a sponsor with money to burn or creating income through camming are only a few of the ways you can survive based on sex appeal. Get creative—the charisma you apply towards women (or men) in the sex arena is the same charisma you will use in the business world to move forward. People do business with people they like—or wish they could fuck. I don't *love* this route to solvency, turning men into thots, but it exists for emergencies.

SELLING YOUR BODY, BUT NOT FOR SEX

I'm beautiful. As poor as I am now, I've got more sex appeal than the entire country of Burundi. But I recognize my fans come in all shapes and sizes, and that not all of you have what it takes to sell yourselves. And that's okay, because selling your body can take many other forms. Practically every industry in America is experiencing a workforce shortage due to Trump's economic revival and a hesitancy to hire illegal aliens for menial labor. They are hiring men with no arms to dig ditches for God's sake. So don't tell me you can't get in the trenches if you need to.

Hard labor will leave you exhausted and dirty but can help you get in shape and is one of nature's best cures for depression—and shame. Besides, who knows what hot moms you can meet bringing shopping carts in from the Safeway parking lot? Of course, your career goals are not to work a shitty dirty job, but you're poor. You need to do whatever you can to generate cash.

I take that back—you need to be a little more selective than blindly picking up jobs. Specifically, you need to avoid the "gig economy" as popularized by Uber, DoorDash, and similar services. You may make some cash driving and delivering, but you'll lose your shirt. All these companies are doing is transferring the cost of vehicles and depreciation to you, the poor sod who thinks you will pull yourself out of poverty by destroying your car.

If you become financially literate enough to understand the wear and tear you're putting on your vehicle by driving around for a billion dollar Silicon Valley company, you'll know you are actually losing money hand over first. The last thing you need to do is make yourself poorer while you think you're gaining ground. Any wear and tear needs to be on your body—sexually or otherwise—and not on your financial assets.

BUT HERE'S HOW THE PROS DO IT

If you want to explore our sexually-charged culture, the best way you can do it is within your marriage. Pleasing your husband or wife and encouraging your children to be healthy and athletic is the optimum path.

The highest value in the sexual marketplace is on the unattainable—people who are off the market. So focus your sexual urges on your spouse and your esthetic urges on your family. There is nothing more wondrous or beautiful than the sight of a family spilling out of church on a Sunday, the mother's hair perfectly teased, the father's tie straight and neatly knotted, and the two sons surging forward, eagerly awaiting their return home and an afternoon of soccer.

VI
DEALING WITH SHAME

Having the wrong kind of friends unquestionably contributed to my financial crash. It was like AOC's Green New Deal, but instead of a ditzy bitch from the suburbs pushing bonkers changes to the American economy to get attention, it was me causing radical changes to the MILO economy by spreading my hard-earned greenbacks around to make my friends happy. Don't worry, I'm not trying to wiggle my way out of responsibility, like a socialist that lectures Americans about cow farts and car emissions while traveling around the world in private jets while her campaign spent nearly as much on Ubers as I used to.

Without question, the money I wasted or flat out lost thanks to "friends" and misguided business adventures pales in comparison to the untold piles of loot I squandered on myself and my lifelong battle with shame. To put it another way, America wasted trillions of dollars fighting endless wars for Israel in the Middle East. All we have to show for it is stirring war footage, videos of family reunions that make people cry, and lots of guys missing body parts who are now at risk for suicide. Not to mention those who never came home. At the risk of offending veterans, *I relate.*

I wasted millions of dollars fighting endless wars against shame, and all I've got to show for it is the shame of being poor. Shame is deadly and apocalyptic if we dwell on it. It is one of the invisible obstacles we must overcome if we are to be part of the short-term poor, and not slip into the hell of long-term poverty. If I weren't so broke, I'd hire a research assistant to help me put together an insightful treatise into shame, with my trademark insightfulness layered on top. But I can't even get a working credit card to hire some tosser on Fiverr, so instead you're going to get my raw emotional take.

Shame is the feeling of humiliation we experience when we do something foolish and realize we are wrong. This is garden-variety shame—an essential component of the human condition. Where would the religions of the world be without us realizing when we've done wrong and feeling bad about it? I guess Islam would still be around chopping heads off willy-nilly, but most other faiths grasp the essential component of saying sorry to our creator, trying to make it right, and doing better in the future.

Think about how normal people feel shame. A fat guy on a diet eats a donut, and five minutes later regrets it. A teenager fails a test after playing Fortnite instead of studying. An employee of Milo Inc, certified as a gun safety expert, leaves multiple AK-47s locked and loaded in several rooms of my mansion where a visitor may shoot themselves or others. What I've experienced throughout my life, leading to countless bad financial decisions, is a type of nuclear-grade shame that makes these examples look completely pathetic. Except perhaps for the gun one—I was sure that employee would get someone killed, but he got laid off first.

Shame led me to make foolish decisions with money in multiple ways. Since I've always felt like an outsider and a weirdo, I used money—or, when I was younger, the illusion of money—to keep people engaged and happy and around me. I wanted people to think I was successful, well-bred, accomplished and a winner because on the inside I felt like the opposite. It wasn't until I found love that I realized my worth and stopped needing these props. It's not a coincidence that this all happened at the same time as Milo Inc was imploding.

Because I hated my parents for neglecting and abandoning me, and because I was embarrassed by both of them, I ended up ashamed of me, too. I knew from an early age I had the power to warp reality when I was speaking to someone and that I could make pretty much anyone believe pretty much anything, so I used it to tell people things about myself that I thought would make them like me more. Eventually, I discovered that was a lot of effort compared to having and spending a lot of money, which had much the same effect.

I have a million examples of bad decisions I've made driven by the need to front or show off, ultimately driven by shame. Although I have been at various points the "kept boy" of wealthy patrons, I in turn acted as a patron to poor young men in an effort to ward off the associated shame. Those men I had sex with were lavished with gifts, and I even looked the other way as they stole things from my house. I even spent inordinately on men I was not having sex with and never would.

Some of these things are already mentioned in this book—cars for young gearheads, high fashion for men who thought America Eagle Outfitters was cutting edge. My shame led me to act like the men I made a living out of mocking, which just created deeper shame, and led to deeper and more ruinous compensation. My financial history is best summarized as a series of vicious cycles becoming increasingly barbarous as the years went by. The sugar daddy dynamic I'd been introduced to in the gay sexual marketplace did something bad to me. It made me think that exercising power and control over other people with money was normal and healthy, and I began to do it myself.

It was retarded. I was professionally making fun of cucks, beta orbiters, and soy boys, while acting as a paypig for straight young guys without father figures. All of this shame was dwarfed by the steady worsening of my financial condition. I may have been financially illiterate, but even I could read the writing on the wall in 2018. As I mentioned earlier, when stockbrokers and CEOs take swan dives from the penthouse, they do it because they understand poverty is coming. While I was never suicidal, I knew poverty was looming, and the shame caused me to squander what little wealth I still had even faster.

Who could imagine that the slings and arrows of outrageous fortune would result in me, the guy who gleefully modeled a shirt that says STOP BEING

POOR being thrown into a personal hell of penury? I love prison sex, but it's so much better outside of prison—thank God there are no longer debtor's prisons. My descent into poverty wasn't a gradual fall, like boiling a frog, or Laura Loomer's 2018 weight gain. It was closer to the aforementioned Titanic... HMS MILO broken in half, not enough lifeboats, and the Irish locked below decks. Other comparable disasters include the U.S. government firing a missile at TWA Flight 800, blowing up the embassy in Benghazi and nuking the Japs (apparently some people still think this was a mistake). By the way, I'm sorry, Laura. I adore you, I just couldn't think of a better joke and I'm on a deadline, and you're in great shape these days.

I had a decision to make. I could continue to kill the shame with drugs and alcohol and I'd end up a bloated fat guy with a bad liver and an addled mind, if I didn't hang myself first. Or I could accept the reality of my new financial situation and fight like hell to save myself so I could get back to helping others and doing the work I was born to do.

MY DECISION

As you can guess based on the fact that you're reading this book, I decided to get off my ass and fight back. This fight has largely been a fight against my shame, which is a lot like depression. Both leave you feeling paralyzed in bed and demoralized. Both make you want to avoid friends, enemies, and everyone in between. Both make the leftist trash on Netflix seem infinitely more interesting than engaging in real world activities that can generate an income. In short, shame and depression can both make an already miserable situation much more miserable, and much less likely to be a short-term situation.

In 2016, I made comments controversial with some portions of my own fan base about depression. I explained the only way to beat it was to work through it. Exercise, do a job—any job—volunteer for a charity, anything to stay active and busy. Some fans argued that depression must be carefully medicated, and great empathy must be extended to the depressed. I explained I had been depressed and got myself out of it—and the formerly depressed agreed with me.

I applied this same logic to the shame I felt about being poor. I addressed it by working as hard as I could on multiple projects, and contributing in other ways like cooking, cleaning, and even doing yard work. I learned the hard way that poor people don't typically have Vietnamese gardeners. I even started answering my own front door!

I also found other ways to deal with uncomfortable feelings. The most powerful tool I have found is a stronger relationship with God. I pray. Mary has helped me every day since I opened myself up to her. Some of you might be recoiling right now from a discussion of religion, because Western culture is training people to turn away from God. But he has rescued me and can rescue you. I also set a modest goal of helping someone every day, even if only in some incredibly minor way. I have helped many thousands of people in my life, I have the emails from people to prove it. Young men who were suicidal until they found motivation in my videos, for example. Somehow I got blown off track and instead of making more videos to help and inspire people I got consumed in the business of being rich and famous. But don't worry. I'm back.

VII
HOW TO STOP BEING POOR

I am the Alpha and the Omega of fearless commentators. I know that the few Americans schools that still taught Greek have since swapped it out for another class on the Holocaust, so I'll forgive you for not knowing that these are the first and last letters of the Greek alphabet.

These days, history lessons are principally concerned with the three women who actually managed to invent something useful. You've never heard of them. Plus, that one black guy in the eighteenth century who fell on a box of crayons and accidentally drew the plans for a condenser mic. So, I'll explain.

When God talks about being the Alpha and the Omega, he means the beginning and end of well... *everything*. I'm not putting myself on His level—well, maybe I am for the purposes of this sentence—but when it comes to speaking truth to power, standing up for vets, college students, gay people, straight people, and everyone else who loves America, I'm it—the only one who never compromises.

I like to compare myself to the Greek hero Achilles. When Achilles was born, his mother dipped him in the river Styx, making him invulnerable everywhere except in the heel she held him by. I've been invulnerable everywhere except my wallet, and perhaps against fake allegations from *National Review* writers that I'm "soft on child abuse."

Taking a stand against progressives and cuck conservatives has cost me terribly. I'm blacklisted or demonetized by practically every tech platform. It's a known fact that half of the shadow-banning and de-ranking techniques developed by Facebook and friends were built from the ground up to shut me up. The rest of the conservative movement came later. If I were a typical poor person, I would blame all these progressive fuckers for my financial collapse. They shut down every revenue stream I had, and they even shut down the email service I was going to use to advertise this book.

It is amazingly easy—and amazingly appealing—to blame my circumstances on others. Not only Silicon Valley, but the scoundrels who bled me dry in business and even in my own house. But I want to be poor temporarily, which begins with taking responsibility. Yes, I faced adversity, but that adversity gave me a *New York Times* bestseller (reliable sources report that four employees were let go for allowing my book to hit the list) and amazing tour events both at home and abroad.

You can summarize my prior interests in life as "Louis, Labels, and Luxury." This isn't a good combination to build wealth, even with an income as formerly outsized as mine. I've done a lot of soul searching on the issue, and believe me, soul searching is a dangerous pastime for a diva like me. You can get lost for days. But it's done me a world of good. By spending hours, often at night, examining myself and my situation, I came to realize what is important to me. Life isn't about "Louis, Labels, and Luxury," it's about something more like: "Faith, Flag, and Family."

I can't bear the sight of America losing its connection to God. Most of black America is still deeply in love with Jesus, of course. Black America goes to church. And although their love of country has been eroded by generations of aggressive race-baiting from the progressive Left, which wrongly associates the idea of America with the persecution and hatred of black skin, and despite some deep social dysfunctions which horribly punish and disadvantage young men—not helped by widespread bias in the criminal justice system—black Americans still, at least, have their faith, which puts them one third of the trifecta ahead of most of you.

I know very few atheists who aren't on medication for anxiety and other mental problems, and I know very few poor atheists who are actively improving their lives. My relationship with God has blossomed to the point where I recorded the beautiful gospel song *Silver and Gold* this year.

National pride and patriotism have always felt natural to me. I love England and my adopted country America. I've been called a racist for this, by neocon midgets and intellectual pygmies. So have you, probably. But pride in your country and your culture is different from a love of government or, worse, a love of one's own race. The proper object of your affections should be the nation, under God. This is one of the things America historically got right. On these shores there was a sense of belonging to a people, despite the best efforts of malign actors from the Left. This unifying force is at risk today like never before as progressives seek to reduce everything to race.

Identifying with other people because you share a sense of the good and agreeing on a basic set of moral principles and, ideally, sharing the same religion, is the best way to organize a society. That religion should of course be Christianity. Patriotism and a shared faith are not gateway drugs to racism. They are the antidote.

Family is something many people take for granted, but I didn't have a family until I had John. He saved me by giving me what all men need to flourish: Responsibility. Knowing that I alone am responsible for keeping food in his belly and a roof over his head have changed me forever. That may be the most shocking truth in this entire book.

Don't think for a moment that this is some sort of sappy redemption arc from one of the cheesy 80s movies I've always loved, like *Shogun Assassin*. Nor is this a conversion story. It's just me telling you how I fixed my priorities, in the hope that what I've learned over the past year or two can help you fix yours. Materialism sent me to the poorhouse. Love, and God, brought me back.

I know you're all still out there. You've been waiting for me to figure this all out. Now I have. I've realized my readers loved me for being witty, charming, devastating to stupid feminists, fearless in my positions, and willing to stand up for them no matter what. Yes, my beautiful hair and face don't hurt—but it isn't the *haute couture* that people come for. It has *never* been about the brands or the luxury. This knowledge has galvanized me for the long fight ahead. I knew I could not let my fans down, because my fans didn't let me down. The outpouring of love and support made it obvious I must continue. And I mean, ugh, there's so much new crazy every day.

In this book I've shared a lot of advice about how to start pulling yourself out of a financial hole. It isn't easy, much of corporate America makes profits hand over fist by ensuring you stay poor—starting with banks charging insane interest rates. But if I can start down the road to fixing my finances, *anyone* can. Remember what MILO has taught you. Stop shoveling your face full of expensive food and drink, and for God's sake, stop smoking—you can't afford it. As your diet improves, make sure you keep exercising. It's the best investment of time and money you can make no matter what your financial situation is. Learn how to get where you need to go on the cheap. No more Uber and Lyft… replace them with friends and family or a bus and bicycle. If a car is strictly necessary, drive the cheapest thing that won't kill you.

Your hair will be the least of your concerns for many of you, but for the few and the proud, you can get the look you want without spending a fortune,

I promise. You will fix your friends list to remove the cunts who love spending your money. They are probably already gone, but just in case, dump them. Keep the people who care about the real you, or better yet, can provide some utility to your life. Start your friend spreadsheet and try to be as ruthless as I have always been.

Critically, you will deal with shame the same way I am. One day at a time, one foot in front of the other. I can't afford to be humble—well, I can't afford anything really—but introducing a bit of humility into your life will do wonders on the road to financial recovery. Learn to act quickly and responsively. If you want to haul yourself out of financial servitude, you'll need to execute tasks almost as blindingly and recklessly quickly as I dashed off this book. Finally, you'll use your body as currency, whether in a sexual manner or in some hard labor or, ideally, within your marriage for noble purposes. It's one of the few things you own outright without a loan against it… so put your assets to work. If you combine all of this advice, you will ensure you are part of the temporary poor instead of the long-term poor.

People who have never fought their weight will have trouble understanding how recovery works. They want a windfall of cash to get back on their feet. I've often struggled with appetite control, so I understand instinctively that the key to success is steady incremental progress. You'll wake up one day with a lot less debt, just like fans who have been inspired by me to lose a lot of weight woke up one day weighing much less than they did a month ago.

While we must all take personal responsibility for our lives, it's worth pointing out that the evils I've warned you against in this book are just some of the many forces ranged against you. Perhaps the most terrifying is the amount of money people borrow these days to spend on things that don't matter or don't even exist. Most Americans are in debt because they took college degrees that are essentially worthless gestures toward status and prestige. Others are buying "virtual goods" on their iPhones on credit cards, using someone else's money to chase a dopamine hit. These are all rabbit holes good people can disappear down.

A lot of it boils down to drug culture, which is everywhere. Take therapy, the cheap substitute for confession, which wants you on antidepressants and paying to see quacks who will help you find new and imaginative reasons you're miserable and locate people to blame. It's a nexus of self-help culture and big pharma from which it's impossible to escape once you've handed over your self-determination to a system that always concludes that you need more pills and more intervention.

What you *should* be doing is identifying what you have done wrong and resolving to fix it, because almost everything that is wrong in your life is within your power to mend. In other words, what you ought to be doing is *confessing your sins.* No sin is more obvious or more widespread in America than that of gluttony. Carbs are a drug that target women especially viciously. And they work just like any other addiction. As you develop glucose resistance, you need sicklier and more disgusting sugary treats to satisfy your cravings. But it works the other way too. You can train yourself into enjoying healthier food. The first few weeks aren't fun, but after three months you literally can't eat the kind of crap you used to without feeling gross. It's all a matter of habit, routine and moderation. (Otherwise known as "Aristotle was right.")

When you give in to one of the seven deadly sins, around which this book's seven chapters are structured, you might feel as though you're indulging yourself. But eventually you realize that you have been enslaving yourself. These things aren't salves. They are poisons. And this is what it means to stop being poor: You must liberate yourself from the things that are holding you to the ground.

I had my own addiction—to buying friendships and admiration and binding people to me with money. Because, for much of my life, I felt unloved and unlovable, I loved those around me recklessly, and did it the easy way, showering affection and gifts. I became a sort of surrogate father to wayward twentysomethings, a strange reimagining of the sugar daddies I'd bled dry in my youth. I thought that being a father meant bribing people to like you. I know now that I must embrace my role as the Prodigal Son and ask my own Heavenly Father for forgiveness and guidance.

It wasn't always obvious to me how deep my own religious convictions ran. But perhaps it should have been. Because where else was I getting the inexhaustible patience, the endless reserves of energy and the unkillable smile? Though I didn't know it at the time, my indefatigability and my unshakeable and infectious joy both sprang from that garden I had not yet fully entered, but which I now explore—and into whose delights I seek to welcome others. That is the purpose of the rest of my life.

I have always felt a keen sense of personal ordination—that I was selected to lead and inspire and do something wonderful with my life. Yet the "alpha male" isn't a classic Christian archetype. Positions of responsibility for Christians do, however, usually mean leadership roles: priests, doctors and teachers. I suppose I've always been a mixture of those three. I have always wanted to help others, and not always known how. Now I know. The harder and better thing is to wage war for the majority.

I will never stop being hysterically brazen on subjects that matter. Most people will still find me grating and outrageous. I will never compromise my positions or dilute my convictions for personal or professional advantage. This will cost me dearly. But it can cost me no more than I have already lost. And the riches I can seize are incalculable. I now realize and can sing honestly and in full throat that I'd rather have a relationship with God and love in my life than earthly possessions—and I say that knowing I'll be fine again in another year or two and the money will be back.

It will relieve many of you to know that I've been feeling an intense desire to return to the subjects and people from which my career first blossomed and about which my readers care the most. I've been reading, preparing, sharpening my claws. I am ready to go to war once again to protect the most precious principles of our civilization. If you thought I was dangerous before, wait until you get a load of me now. I am never going away for one simple reason. I won't give those bastards the satisfaction. Come hell or high water, ban or blockade, I'll be here, laughing and waging war for what matters until the day I drop dead. And if John's driving a Lamborghini Huracán instead of a Bugatti, well, I'll just have to make it up to him some other way.

ABOUT THE AUTHOR

Milo Yiannopoulos is an award-winning journalist, a *New York Times*-bestselling author, an international political celebrity, a free speech martyr, a comedian, an accomplished entrepreneur, a hair icon, a penitent and, to the annoyance of his many enemies, an exceedingly happy person. He is the most censored, most lied-about man in the world, banned from stepping foot on entire continents for his unapologetic commitment to free expression. But he is also one of the most sought-after speakers anywhere, invited by foreign governments, wealthy individuals and even the occasional courageous private company to share his unique blend of laughter and war. Milo lurches from improbable triumph to improbable triumph, loathed by establishment Left and Right alike. His first book, *Dangerous*, sold over 200,000 copies, despite never being reviewed in any major publication. Milo lives in New Jersey with his husband, John.

CPSIA information can be obtained
at www.ICGtesting.com
Printed in the USA
LVHW092222150419
614298LV00001B/2/P